FOUR CORNERS

Second Edition Workbook

JACK C. RICHARDS & DAVID BOHLKE

CAMBRIDGE
UNIVERSITY PRESS

CAMBRIDGE
UNIVERSITY PRESS

University Printing House, Cambridge CB2 8BS, United Kingdom

One Liberty Plaza, 20th Floor, New York, NY 10006, USA

477 Williamstown Road, Port Melbourne, VIC 3207, Australia

314–321, 3rd Floor, Plot 3, Splendor Forum, Jasola District Centre, New Delhi – 110025, India

103 Penang Road, #05-06/07, Visioncrest Commercial, Singapore 238467

Cambridge University Press is part of the University of Cambridge.

It furthers the University's mission by disseminating knowledge in the pursuit of education, learning and research at the highest international levels of excellence.

www.cambridge.org
Information on this title: www.cambridge.org/fourcorners

© Cambridge University Press 2012, 2019

First published 2012
Second edition 2019

20 19 18 17 16 15 14 13 12 11 10 9 8 7 6 5 4 3

Printed in Poland by Opolgraf

A catalogue record for this publication is available from the British Library

ISBN 978-1-108-55989-8 Student's Book with Online Self-Study 4
ISBN 978-1-108-55990-4 Student's Book with Online Self-Study 4A
ISBN 978-1-108-63118-1 Student's Book with Online Self-Study 4B
ISBN 978-1-108-56025-2 Student's Book with Online Self-Study and Online Workbook 4
ISBN 978-1-108-56029-0 Student's Book with Online Self-Study and Online Workbook 4A
ISBN 978-1-108-56032-0 Student's Book with Online Self-Study and Online Workbook 4B
ISBN 978-1-108-45942-6 Workbook 4
ISBN 978-1-108-45945-7 Workbook 4A
ISBN 978-1-108-45946-4 Workbook 4B
ISBN 978-1-108-64434-1 Teacher's Edition with Complete Assessment Program 4
ISBN 978-1-108-56022-1 Full Contact with Online Self-Study 4
ISBN 978-1-108-56023-8 Full Contact with Online Self-Study 4A
ISBN 978-1-108-56024-5 Full Contact with Online Self-Study 4B
ISBN 978-1-108-45952-5 Presentation Plus Level 4

Additional resources for this publication at www.cambridge.org/fourcorners

Contents

Credits

The news

A Stories in the news

1 **Match the news sections to the headlines.**

1 New Cell Phones in Stores Today ___d___   a Travel

2 Singer Wins Music Award _____   b Entertainment

3 Big Storm Coming to New York _____   c Sports

4 Food Can Make You Sick _____   d Technology / Science

5 Big Company Closes _____   e Health

6 Soccer Player Makes Six Goals _____   f Weather

7 Cheap Vacations in Australia _____   g Business

2 **Circle TWO stories that would be in each news section.**

1 Lifestyle

   (a) a story about a new restaurant that people are going to

   b a story about a new cell phone and how it works

   c a story about what people like to do on weekends

2 Local

   a a story about a school and its students

   b a story about problems in a small town

   c a story about a singer's tour around the world

3 World

   a a story about a storm in seven countries

   b a story about companies around the world

   c a weather report for San Diego, California

3 Look at the chart. Then write sentences about the people. Use the past continuous and the present continuous.

Name	When the storm started	Right now
Melvin	work on his computer	watch the storm
Tim	read a good book	finish the book
Susana	drive to Austin	visit her friends there
Emma	shop	take the bus home
Mr. and Mrs. Lee	walk to the park	sit at home
Shelly and Frank	ride their bikes	eat at a restaurant

1 When the storm started, Melvin _was working on his computer_ . **Now** _he is watching the storm_ .

2 Tim _____ . Now _____ .

3 Susana _____ . Now _____ .

4 Emma _____ . Now _____ .

5 Mr. and Mrs. Lee _____ . Now _____ .

6 Shelly and Frank _____ . Now _____ .

4 Circle the correct verb forms to complete the conversation.

Jay   Did you hear about what happened last night?

Jorge Morena **makes** / **(made)** six goals in the game!

                        ₁

Becky Wow! Did you see it on TV?

Jay   No, but I **read** / **'m reading** about it in the

              ₂

paper today.

Becky But wait. Morena **hasn't played** / **didn't play**

                           ₃

since he hurt his leg last year.

Jay   Well, he **played** / **has played** last night, and I'm sure he

                    ₄

won / **will win** MVP this year.

     ₅

Becky MVP? What's that?

Jay   It **means** / **is meaning** Most Valuable Player. It's the award for the best player

               ₆

on the team.

Becky Hmm . . . MVP after only one good game?

Jay   No, he **is** / **was** a great player before he hurt his leg. He **has had** / **had** a great

              ₇   ₈

career for more than ten years, and he's still great!

Becky I can't believe I **haven't heard** / **will hear** more about him. I **will watch** / **watch** him

                                     ₉   ₁₀

in the future!

5 Complete the text with the correct form of the verbs in parentheses. Use the simple present, the simple past, or the future with *will*.

KSmart: Personal Tech Review by Justin Wilson

The new smartphone, KSmart by SMT, _____is_____ (be) in
1

stores today. I _____ (think) it's a pretty good phone
2

for the money. The KSmart _____ (have) a lot of great
3

features, like a fingerprint sensor. The older version of the phone, the JSmart,

_____ (not have) a fingerprint sensor. The KSmart
4

_____ (come) with many great apps, and the company
5

_____ (offer) classes in the future on how to use all of
6

them.

SMT _____ (give) me a phone to test last week. Right
7

now, there _____ (be) a few problems. For example, the wireless charger
8

_____ (not work) well. The company has said they _____
9   10

(fix) the problem soon.

Even with a few problems, I think the KSmart _____ (be) SMT's most
11

popular phone this year. The JSmart _____ (not be) a great phone,
12

but the KSmart _____ (be) fantastic!
13

6 Answer the questions with your own information. Use complete sentences.

Example: __My favorite restaurant is Taco King.__

1 What's your favorite restaurant? _____

2 Is it popular? When is it the busiest? _____

3 What kind of food does the restaurant serve? _____

4 How many times have you been there? _____

5 Who do you usually go there with? _____

6 When was the last time you went? What did you eat? _____

7 What other foods have you eaten there? _____

8 Will you eat there again soon? _____

B I totally agree.

1 Complete each conversation with the correct sentence from the box.

> I couldn't agree with you more.   I'm not sure about that.

1 **Diana** Hey, Joe. Did you hear about the water problem in Clinton?

   Joe I read about it yesterday. I don't think it's a big problem.

   Diana _____ .

           It seems pretty awful to me.

> I'm not sure that's really true.   I totally agree.

2 **Yawen** This radio program is great. I think the radio is the best way to get news.

   Vicky _____ .

   Yawen Really?

   Vicky I think getting news on the Internet is better. You can listen to it or read it.

> I don't know about that.   I feel exactly the same way.

3 **Henry** Look at this, Laura. Bruno Mars will be at the Music Center next month.

   Laura Let's go hear him! He's a great singer.

   Henry _____ . I love his music.

2 Complete the conversations with your own ideas. Use some of the expressions from the boxes in Exercise 1.

Example: I couldn't agree with you more.

1 **Friend** I think pollution is the biggest problem in our city.

   You _____

2 **Friend** I think the best way to get the news is on TV.

   You _____

3 **Friend** Let's go to an Alessia Cara concert. She's the best singer!

   You _____

C Survival stories

1 Complete the puzzle with the correct verbs that complete the headlines. What's the mystery word?

1 Man _____ Three Days in Ocean

2 Plane _____ into Zoo – No Animals Hurt

3 Mountain Lion _____ Hiker – Hiker Survives

4 Dog _____ Boy Up Tree

5 Car _____ – No One Hurt

6 Storm Coming – _____ Local Beach

7 Lightning Hits House But _____ New Library

```
    1  S  U  R  V  I  V  E  S
 2
 3
             4
 5
        6
        7
```

2 Write the correct headline from Exercise 1 under each picture.

1 _Storm Coming – Threatens Local Beach_

2 _____

3 _____

4 _____

3 Complete the conversation with the correct form of the verb in parentheses. Use the simple past, the past continuous, the present perfect, or the future with *will*.

Reporter Today, I'm speaking with Brandon Nelson. He survived three days in the ocean without food. Brandon, what happened?

Brandon Well, I was on my boat alone, and there was a storm.

Reporter Where _____were_____ you _____going_____ (go)?
   1   1

Brandon I was sailing from California to Australia.

Reporter That's a big trip. You must have experience. How long _____ you _____ (be) a sailor?
   2   2

Brandon I've sailed since I was a child.

Reporter What _____ you _____ (do) when the storm hit?
   3   3

Brandon I was preparing the boat for the storm, but it was too late. Suddenly a big wave overturned the boat. The boat broke into pieces, and I was in the water.

Reporter How _____ you _____ (survive)?
   4   4

Brandon At first, I didn't think I would survive. But I found a piece of my boat in the ocean, and I held onto it.

Reporter What _____ you _____ (eat)?
   5   5

Brandon I didn't eat! I found some bottles of water in the ocean that came off the boat in the storm.

Reporter Wow! You drank only water for three days! So finally some other sailors found you. How _____ you _____ (feel) then?
   6   6

Brandon Well, of course, I was very, very happy!

Reporter _____ you ever _____ (go) on a boat again?
   7   7

Brandon Oh, yes. I hurt my arm, but as soon as it's better, I'll go sailing again.

Reporter What _____ you _____ (do) differently?
   8   8

Brandon Well, I probably won't go alone again.

Reporter That's a good idea! Well, Brandon, thank you for telling us your story.

4 Complete the conversation by writing Ms. Rivera's questions with the words in parentheses. Use Ms. Hill's answers to help you.

Ms. Rivera   So, _have you been here before_ ?
                 1
               (you / be / here before)

Ms. Hill   No, I haven't. It's my first time here.

Ms. Rivera   Well, _____
                      2
        _____ ?
                      2
        (how / you / hear / about us)

Ms. Hill   My friend Sandra Bern told me about you.

Ms. Rivera   Wonderful. So, _____
                      3
        _____ ? (how / you / feel / today)
            3

Ms. Hill   I'm feeling sick to my stomach.

Ms. Rivera   I'm sorry. _____ ?
                      4
        (when / you / get / sick)

Ms. Hill   I got sick last week.

Ms. Rivera   _____ ?
                      5
        (you / be / to another doctor before today)

Ms. Hill   No, I haven't.

Ms. Rivera   _____ ?
                      6
        (you / take / any medication)

Ms. Hill   No, I'm not taking anything.

Ms. Rivera   OK, thank you. The doctor will see you soon. Oh,
        _____ ?
                      7
        (how / you / pay / today)

Ms. Hill   I'll pay with a credit card if that's OK.

5 Read the situations. Then answer the questions with your own ideas.

Example: _I close the windows, and I turn on the radio._

1   There is a big storm and you are at home. What do you do? _____

2   A bear is chasing you. What are you doing? _____

3   You have been lost in the mountains for two days. You have a little water and a sandwich.
    How will you survive? _____

4   A shark threatened a beach last week. You are at the beach today. Do you swim
    in the ocean? Why or why not? _____

D Creating news

1 Read the article. Write what the letters mean.

1 JNW _____ 2 SMS _____

SMS NEWS

JASMINE NEWS (JNW) gives people in Sri Lanka, an island country south of India, a new way to get news. It sends news headlines to people in text messages on their cell phones. The text messages are short and give people information about important events. JNW is getting news to people faster than radio, television, and even the Internet.

SMS stands for "Short Message Service," and it's the system used for text messages. JNW started in 2006, and then in 2007, JNW started working with a phone company to send SMS news. It was the first company in Sri Lanka, and one of the first companies in Asia, to use SMS news. JNW is using new technology and working with phone services so that people can get the news with any type of phone. Although SMS news is shorter than other types of news stories, JNW has high standards. They want all of their headlines to be correct and neutral. They check all information with at least three sources, like different people and newspapers. If they make a mistake, they quickly send a text with the correct information.

JNW feels the most important part of their service is sharing the news, opinions, and experiences of Sri Lanka's citizens. They report news about what citizens want and need. They have journalists who report the news in three languages – Sinhala and Tamil, two of the languages spoken in Sri Lanka, and English. JNW also uses citizen journalists and gets some news from everyday citizens.

It does cost money to get SMS news, but JNW thinks it's important that anyone who wants it can get it. They have a pay-what-you-can program for people who can't afford the regular price.

2 Read the text again. Then answer the questions.

1 How do people get news from JNW? _on their cell phones / in text messages_

2 When did JNW start sending SMS news? _____

3 What does JNW do to make sure headlines are correct? _____

4 What does JNW do if they make a mistake? _____

5 In what languages does JNW report the news? _____

Communicating

A Language learning

Put the letters in the correct order to make sentences.

1 h a t w c / i o n e l n / d e v i o / p c l s i /. <u>Watch online video clips.</u>

2 l k t a / o t / e r s y l u o f / u o t / d l o u /. _____

3 p e e k / a / a r v c a l o y u b / n b e k o o o t /. _____

4 h w t a c / s m v e o i / t i w h / t s s l i u t b e /. _____

5 l k t a / t w h i / e a v t n i / a p s e r s e k /. _____

6 e m k a / h l s f a / d s c a r /. _____

2 **Look at the pictures. Write sentences with language-learning tips.**

1 <u>She watches online video clips.</u>

2 _____

3 _____

4 _____

5 _____

6 _____

3 Check (✓) the correct sentences. Then change the sentences that are NOT correct to the present perfect.

1 ☐ I've been knowing Tom for ten years. <u>I've known Tom for ten years.</u>

2 ☑ Jill has been keeping a vocabulary notebook recently. _____

3 ☐ We've been driving this car for about two years. _____

4 ☐ Lola has been owning her bicycle for a long time. _____

5 ☐ Su Ho hasn't been belonging to our club very long. _____

6 ☐ I've been watching online video clips all day. _____

7 ☐ They have never been believing my story. _____

8 ☐ How long have you been waiting here? _____

4 Complete the email with the present perfect continuous. Use the words in parentheses.

Hi Rafa,

<u>Have you been having</u> (you / have) a good time in summer school? Which classes are
    1
you taking? I'm not taking summer classes this year, but _____ (I / practice)
                                                                                          2
my English a lot lately. _____ (I / live) in Toronto, Canada, this
                                    3
summer, and _____ (I / talk) with native speakers every day.
                        4
_____ (I / watch) a lot of movies recently, but
        5
_____ (I / not watch) them with subtitles. My English
        6
is improving, so I can understand the movies without the subtitles!

Do you have Mr. Payton for English again? _____ (he / use)
                                                                          7
PowerPoint presentations in class? _____ (the class / watch) any
                                                            8
TED talks? If yes, please send me the titles of the talks.

_____ (I / not use) my tablet computer because it isn't working.
        9
I came to an Internet café to send you this email. I hope you're having a good summer.

Your friend,

Carla

P.S. _____ (I / take) a lot of pictures.
            10
    Look at the streetcar!

5 Look at the chart. Then answer the questions.

	Talks with native speakers	Watches online video clips in English	Keeps a vocabulary notebook
Tina	✓	✓	✓
Caroline		✓	✓
Marcos	✓		✓
Andrew	✓		

1 Has Tina been watching online videos in English?   Yes, she has.
2 Have Tina and Marcos been keeping vocabulary notebooks?   _____
3 Has Caroline been talking with native speakers?   _____
4 Has Marcos been talking with native speakers?   _____
5 Have Marcos and Andrew been watching online videos in English?   _____
6 Has Andrew been keeping a vocabulary notebook?   _____

6 Look at the answers. Write the questions. Use the underlined words to help you.

1 A   What have you been studying?
  B I've been studying English.
2 A   _____
  B I've been studying English for five years.
3 A   _____
  B I've been taking classes at Monroe Language School.
4 A   _____
  B I've been practicing English by reading in English.
5 A   _____
  B I've been reading magazines lately.

7 Answer the questions with your own information. Use complete sentences.

Example: Yes, I have. I've been studying English for three years.

1 Have you been studying English for very long? How long?

  _____

2 Have you been reading in English? What have you been reading recently?

  _____

3 Has your teacher been giving you homework lately? How much?

  _____

B One possibility is . . .

1 Read each sentence. Then write E (expressing interest) or O (offering options).

1 One possibility is reading a lot of books and magazines. _____O_____

2 How about watching movies with subtitles? _____

3 I'm trying to find a way to improve my vocabulary. _____

4 I'm interested in improving my listening comprehension. _____

5 You might want to look in a local newspaper or online. _____

6 I'm looking for a conversation group. _____

2 Complete the conversations with the sentences from Exercise 1.

A. **Albert**   What are you doing, Julia?

   Julia   _I'm looking for a conversation group_____ .

1

   I thought there might be information in this magazine.

   Albert   Hmm . . . I don't know if you'll find information
   on a conversation group in a magazine.

   _____ .

2

   Julia   I'll look online! Thanks.

B. **Ji Ah**   Excuse me, Dana. Can you help me?

   Dana   Sure, Ji Ah.

   Ji Ah   I wrote the word *very* in my paper too many times.

   _____ .

1

   Dana   _____ .

2

   You can learn new words and write them in a notebook.

   Ji Ah   Hey, that's a great idea.

C. **Mr. Wei**   So, Atakan, how can I help you today?

   Atakan   Well, _____ .

1

   I listen to English music, but my listening skills aren't getting better.

   Mr. Wei   I'm not surprised. Music is difficult to understand.

   _____ ?

2

   Try to listen first, and then read the subtitles if you still don't understand what you heard.

   Atakan   That's a good idea, Mr. Wei. Thank you.

C Have her message me.

1 Complete the conversations with the phrases from the box.

answer the phone	left her a voice message	screen my calls
call my mother back	✓ let the call go to voice mail	turn off my phone
don't check voice mail	respond to an email	update your status online
ignored my text		

A. **Kim** Well, if you think the job interview went well, you . . .

   Doug Sorry, Kim. My phone is ringing.

   Kim Could you please ___let the call go to voice mail___ ?

1
   You can call the person back after dinner.

   Doug No! I really have to _____ !

2
   It might be about the job.

B. **Hiro** Is Wendy coming to the party on Friday?

   Eric I don't know. She _____ .

1

   Hiro Hmm . . . Well, maybe she would _____ .

2

   Eric Yeah. I'll email her tonight.

C. **Jen** I'll be right back, Mike. I have to _____ .

1

   Mike OK. Tell your mom "hi."

   . . .

   Mike That was fast.

   Jen She didn't answer the phone, so I _____ .

2

D. **Lilly** I could never work at home. How do you get so much work done, Kyle?

   Kyle Well, I _____ , and I only answer calls about work.

1
   And I _____ until the end of the day.

2

   Lilly Really? I check mine every five minutes!

   Kyle Not me. And if I'm really busy, I _____ .

3
   I also don't use the Internet. I mean, I only use it for work!

   Lilly Wow. You're really dedicated. When do you _____ ?

4

   Kyle I usually update it in the evening.

2 Answer the questions with your own information. Use complete sentences.

Example: People should turn off their cell phones in restaurants because other
              people don't want to hear them talking.

1   Do you think people should turn off their cell phones in restaurants?
    Why or why not?

    _____

2   How often do you check your voice mail?

    _____

3   What else can you do on your cell phone?

    _____

4   Do you screen your calls on your cell phone? When?

    _____

5   Have you answered your phone in class recently? What happened?

    _____

6   Do you think there is ever a good reason to ignore a text? If yes, when?

    _____

3 Put the words in the correct order to make sentences.

1   have / Would / Jenny / call me / tomorrow / you / ?
    Would you have Jenny call me tomorrow?

2   them / to the party / ask / you / come / Did / to / ?

    _____

3   vocabulary / learn / me / help / new / you / Will / ?

    _____

4   phone / her / let / use / me / today / Mindy / .

    _____

5   his / to / soccer game / go / invited us / to / Dan / .

    _____

6   going / take the bus / Are / make / to / you / them / ?

    _____

7   be / tell / to / Don't / quiet / me / !

    _____

8   next week / remind / I'll / to / the information / email / you / .

    _____

4 Complete the sentences with the correct form of the verb in parentheses.

> Paula,
>
> Thanks for staying with Lisa and Mark. Here are a few reminders:
>
> - Remind Lisa _____ *to take out* _____ (take out) the garbage.
>   1
> - Help Mark _____ (do) his homework every night.
>   2
> - You can let Lisa and Mark _____ (have) friends at
>   3
>   the house, but only on the weekends.
> - Mark invited his soccer coach _____ (come) for
>   4
>   dinner on Friday. You can order Chinese food.
> - Have Lisa or Mark _____ (call) me every night!
>   5
> - Make them _____ (go) to bed by 10:00 p.m.
>   6
> - If you can't find something, ask Lisa _____ (help) you.
>   7
> - Oh, and tell them _____ (clean) the house before I get home.
>   8
>
> ☺ Yasmin

5 Circle the correct word to complete each sentence.

1 Could you (ask)/ **have** Tom to respond to my email?

2 Larry won't **invite** / **let** me help him with his homework.

3 Have they been **helping** / **asking** you make flash cards?

4 Mary **made** / **invited** me to join her conversation group.

5 Please **let** / **tell** Jenna to update her online status.

6 Mr. Kent has been **making** / **telling** his students keep vocabulary notebooks.

7 Did the teachers **remind** / **have** the students turn off their cell phones?

6 Answer the questions with your own information. Use a verb followed by an object and another base verb or infinitive.

Example: _Yes, I have. I helped my grandfather respond to an email._

1 Have you ever helped someone with a computer problem? Who?

_____

2 Have you ever let someone help you with a problem? What problem?

_____

3 Have you ever told someone not to call you? Who?

_____

D Modern communication

1 Read the article. Who is the fastest texter in the world?

TEXT IT TO ME!

The first text message was sent in 1992, and texting has become extremely popular since that time. There are about 7.6 billion people in the world, and in 2015, about 23 billion text messages were sent every day. It's a popular way to communicate around the world.

The United States

Text messaging is very popular in the United States. In the past, it was mainly popular with people ages 13 to 22, but today, many older people are sending texts, too. People use it to communicate with friends, and it's being used for business, too. Many airlines are sending text messages to people to remind them to check in for their flights.

Finland

In Finland, there are text-messaging game shows on TV. People watch TV and get quiz questions. They text the answers to the TV station. The person who texts the most correct answers wins!

The Philippines

Some people used to call the Philippines the text capital of the world. Today, with easier internet access and more smartphones, some say the country has become the most social nation. There are over 107 thousand cell phones, and texting is very popular because it is cheap and reliable. People even use text messaging to share opinions about politics and the news.

Japan, China, and South Korea

Japan was one of the first countries to use text messages to communicate. In China, sending text messages is the most popular way to communicate. It's cheaper than talking on the phone. There's a problem in China with "spam" texts, unwanted messages sent to a lot of people at the same time. Spam email is a problem in many countries; in China, it's a problem with text messages, too. Many South Koreans use text messaging, and some of the fastest texters are from South Korea.

Brazil

Brazilians love to text, but texting is less popular than in Europe or the United States. This is because phone plans are fairly expensive and sometimes do not have messaging services. It is more popular to use social media such as Facebook to send messages. In 2014, Marcel Fernandes Filho from Brazil broke the Guinness World Record as the fastest texter in the world.

2 Read the text again. Then write the country.

1 Marcel broke a 2014 world texting record. _____ Brazil _____

2 Texting is used for quiz shows. _____

3 People text each other about politics. _____

4 You can get a text with flight information. _____

5 This country was one of the first to use text messages to communicate. _____

6 Getting spam texts is a problem. _____

Food

A Street food

1 Complete the recipes with the correct verbs for food preparation.

Easy Dumplings

Fill the dough with chicken or beef.

Boil_____ the dumplings for
          1
10 minutes or s_____ them for
                    2
about 20 minutes. Serve them right away
with a good soup.

Fantastic Chicken

Put chicken, small potatoes, and carrots
in a pan. Ba_____ or
                3
r_____ them for about one
     4
hour and 30 minutes. Serve with a
green salad.

Simple Stir-Fry

Cut up the chicken and put it with
vegetables and soy sauce in a hot pan.
F_____ them for 10 to 12
     5
minutes. To enjoy the stir-fry the next
day, m_____ it for one minute
               6
on high.

Super Burgers

For a fast meal, make Super Burgers.
G_____ hamburgers for about
     7
8 to 10 minutes, turning once.
M_____ cheese on the burgers
     8
for the last minute. Serve on a bun with
lettuce and tomato.

2 Circle the correct words to complete each sentence.

1   Hot dogs _____ on the streets in New York City.

   (a) are sold   b are sell   c sells

2   They _____ by hundreds of people.

   a are buying   b are bought   c bought

3   The hot dogs _____ , not fried.

   a boils   b is boiled   c are boiled

4   Water _____ by vendors, too.

   a are sold   b is sold   c is selling

5   The bottles of water _____ in cold water.

   a is kept   b are keeping   c are kept

6   The hot dog carts _____ at the end of each day.

   a is moved   b are moving   c are moved

3 Read the sentences. Write A (active) or P (passive).

1   Five different desserts are served at my favorite restaurant. ____P____

2   The vegetables are steamed, but the fish is fried. _____

3   They make the soup at the restaurant, and they serve it with a salad. _____

4   The fruit is served cold on ice cream. _____

5   The chef grills chicken and beef at your table. _____

6   The hot dogs for the company parties are bought from a vendor. _____

7   The waiter makes the salad at your table. _____

8   The cooks fry the empanadas in the morning, and they microwave them before serving. _____

9   He bakes the cake for 40 minutes. _____

4 Change the active sentences in Exercise 3 to the present passive.

1   The soup is made at the restaurant, and it is served with a salad.

2   _____

3   _____

4   _____

5   _____

5 Complete the text with the present passive of the verbs in parentheses.

MARTY'S FINE FOOD

Come to our new restaurant on Maple Street.

- You'll love our exotic menu! The seafood is local.

  It _is brought_ (bring) to our restaurant
  1
  three times a week.

- Our bread _____ (bake) fresh
  2
  every morning.

- Our vegetables _____ (grow)
  3
  on local, organic farms.

- Breakfast _____ (serve) from
  4
  8:00 a.m. to 11:30 a.m.

- Lunch and dinner _____ (serve) all day.
  5

- Prices _____ (list) on our website.
  6
  See www.martysfinefood/cup.com.

Please visit us soon and let us make you a great meal!

6 Answer the questions with your own ideas. Write complete sentences with
the present passive.

Example: _Hamburgers and dumplings are often fried._

1 What are two foods that are often fried?

_____

2 What are three foods that are served at your favorite restaurant?

_____

3 What is one food that is often melted on hamburgers?

_____

4 What are two foods that are boiled?

_____

5 What is one food that is baked?

_____

6 What is one food that is steamed?

_____

B Sounds good to me.

1 Write the conversation in the correct order.

> Then if I were you, I'd get the lamb chops.
>
> That's a good idea.
>
> I know. What are you going to have?
>
> OK. I think I'll do that. Why don't you get the lamb chops, too?
>
> ✓ This new restaurant is great. There are so many things on the menu.
>
> Why don't you try the cheese ravioli?

Kari   *This new restaurant is great. There are so many things on the menu.*

John _____

Kari   Everything looks good. I have no idea what to get.

John _____

Kari   No, I had pasta for lunch.

John _____

Kari _____

John _____

2 Complete the conversation with the phrases from the box and food from the menu.

> Sounds good to me.   My recommendation would be to . . .

MARTY'S FINE FOOD
Main Dishes

Lamb Chops	$21.00
Cheese Ravioli	$13.00
Baked Fish	$16.00
Grilled Steak	$16.00

Friend   Everything looks good. I don't know what to get.

You _____

Friend _____

C Mix and bake

1 Circle the correct words to complete the conversations.

Luz	Let's get popcorn. OK?
Gi Woo	No, it's too (salty) / sour. How about some lemon candy?
Luz	That's too **creamy** / **sour** for me! Cotton candy?
Gi Woo	Too **crunchy** / **sticky**. How about the Fruit Chews?
Luz	Great. They're **juicy** / **salty** and wonderful!

Mei Do you want a pretzel? They're really **chewy** / **sweet**.

Lori No, thanks. I think they're **bland** / **sticky**. They don't have any taste.

Mei How about a chocolate cookie? They're **salty** / **sweet**.

Lori That sounds great, thanks.

Ming Do you like the chili?

Raul Well, it's really **creamy** / **crunchy**, but it's too **bland** / **spicy** for me. I mean, it tastes good, but it has too much red pepper in it! How are the tacos?

Ming They're great. They're **chewy** / **crunchy**, and they're not spicy at all.

2 Write the cooking directions in the correct order on the recipe card. Do the rice first.
Then do the beans.

Rice
After it boils, cover the pan and turn down the heat.
Cook it for 15 more minutes or until the water is gone.
✓ Put the water and rice in a pan.
Once it is cooked, put it in a bowl until the beans are finished.
Then cook the rice until it boils.

Beans
As soon as they're done, pour them over the rice.
Then turn down the heat, and boil the beans for about 1½ hours.
Once it boils, add the beans and a little salt.
Put some water in a pan, and heat it until it boils.

Ruth's Rice and Beans Recipe

Ingredients for Rice:	Ingredients for Beans:
350 ml water	1 liter water
225 grams rice	500 grams red beans
	salt

Before you cook, clean the beans and put them in cold water for 8 to 12 hours.
Then pour off the water and put the beans in the refrigerator.

To start cooking, make the rice.

1   Put the water and rice in a pan.

2   _____

3   _____

4   _____

5   _____

While the rice is cooking, start the beans.

6   _____

7   _____

8   _____

9   _____

Serve hot.

3 Circle the correct words to complete the email.

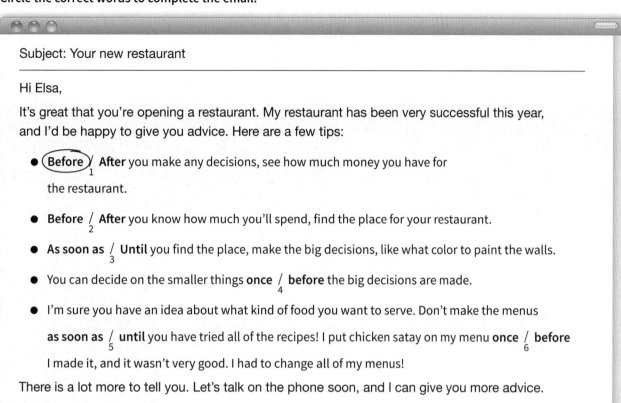

Subject: Your new restaurant

Hi Elsa,

It's great that you're opening a restaurant. My restaurant has been very successful this year, and I'd be happy to give you advice. Here are a few tips:

- **(Before)** / **After** you make any decisions, see how much money you have for
  1
  the restaurant.

- **Before** / **After** you know how much you'll spend, find the place for your restaurant.
  2

- **As soon as** / **Until** you find the place, make the big decisions, like what color to paint the walls.
  3

- You can decide on the smaller things **once** / **before** the big decisions are made.
  4

- I'm sure you have an idea about what kind of food you want to serve. Don't make the menus
  as soon as / **until** you have tried all of the recipes! I put chicken satay on my menu **once** / **before**
  5   6
  I made it, and it wasn't very good. I had to change all of my menus!

There is a lot more to tell you. Let's talk on the phone soon, and I can give you more advice.

Marty

4 Write a simple recipe for a food you know. Use time clauses with some of the words in the box.

| after | as soon as | before | once | until |

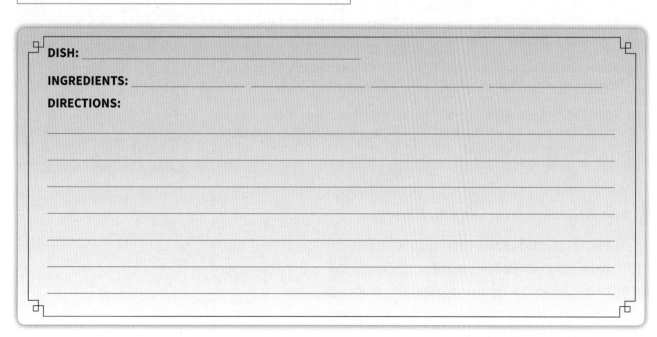

DISH: _____

INGREDIENTS: _____ _____ _____ _____

DIRECTIONS:

_____

_____

_____

_____

_____

_____

D Future food

1 Read the article. How long do you have to wait before you can eat the cake?

a 20 minutes   b 40 minutes   c 60 minutes

Chocolate Dream Cake
by Mari Park

A delicious cake that's easy to make!

225 grams flour
225 grams sugar
75 grams cocoa powder
1 teaspoon baking soda

1 tablespoon butter, melted
80 ml oil
250 ml cold water

Before you add the liquids, mix the dry ingredients together. Once they are mixed, add the butter and oil. Pour the cold water into the mixture and stir. Bake in a round pan for 40 minutes. Let cool for 20 minutes before you serve it.

COMMENTS: + Post a comment

DiPeters26 This cake was easy to make, and it was delicious! I added a chocolate sauce over the top of the cake. Delicious!

MarcosG I made this cake, and I thought it was too bland. It needs a little salt. And DiPeters26, can you give me your sauce recipe?

DiPeters26 Sure, MarcosG. Mix 225 grams of powdered sugar, 2 teaspoons of butter, 1 teaspoon of vanilla, 200 grams of cocoa, and 125 ml of milk. Boil together until sauce starts to get thick. Then cool and pour over cake.

KloveCook I tried this recipe, but the cake was too dry. Next time, I might add more butter. I think I'll try DiPeters26's chocolate sauce, too.

MTP1987 This cake was great! My only problem was that it was too small. The next time, I doubled the recipe and baked it in two pans. My family loves this cake!

OTHER RECIPES:
No Bake Cookies
Double Chocolate
   Cake
Apple Cobbler
Mini Chocolate
   Cookies
Chocolate Surprise
Cocoa Cream Puffs
Easy Frosting

VIDEOS:
How to Make
   Healthy Desserts
How to Sift Flour
Where to Buy Good
   Chocolate

2 Read the text again. Then write T (true) or F (false).

1   For the cake, you add the butter last. ___F___

2   You boil the water before you add it. _____

3   MarcosG doesn't want the chocolate sauce recipe. _____

4   KloveCook hasn't tried DiPeters26's chocolate sauce yet. _____

5   MTP1987 made the cake more than once. _____

Behavior

A The right thing to do

1 Match the two parts of each phrase.

1 give ___b___   a in line
2 keep _____   b someone a gift
3 cut _____   c someone waiting
4 talk _____   d loudly in public

5 offer _____   e litter
6 admit _____   f a mistake
7 drop _____   g someone your seat
8 give _____   h someone a compliment

2 Complete each conversation with a kind of polite or impolite behavior.

1 A Excuse me, you can't _cut in line_____ .
     I was here first.

   B Oh, I'm sorry. I didn't see you.

2 A You should _____ that woman
     _____ . She has a lot of bags.

   B Good idea. I don't mind standing on the subway, and
     she needs the seat.

3 A Hey, you shouldn't _____
     on the street. It's not good for the environment.

   B Yeah, you're right. I'll pick it up.

4 A You really shouldn't _____ on your cell phone.
     It's impolite. I'm trying to listen to the music.

   B Sorry. I'll go to another place to talk.

5 A John can never _____ . He always says
     he's right.

   B I know, but he's really wrong this time.

6 A In the United States, do you _____ a friend _____
     for the Fourth of July?

   B No, but if you go to a Fourth of July party, you could take some food.

3 Complete the interview with the correct sentences from the box.

> ✓ And what would you do if something bad happened?
> I guess I'd like to be an astronaut!
> No, I wouldn't.
> What would you do if someone got sick?
> What would you do if you weren't a pilot?

Reporter I'm talking to pilot Tonya Hitchcock. So, Captain Hitchcock, have you ever been in a dangerous situation?

Tonya No, I really haven't.

Reporter <u>And what would you do if something bad happened?</u>
1

Tonya Well, I'd stay calm and try to find a solution.

Reporter That's a good plan. Now, has anyone ever gotten really sick on the plane?

Tonya No, not on one of my flights.

Reporter _____
2
Would you turn the plane around?

Tonya _____
3
First, I'd ask if there were a doctor on the plane!

Reporter That's a good idea. One last question.

_____
4

Tonya Hmm . . . another job? _____
5

4 Put the words in the correct order to make sentences.

1 be angry / I'd / someone / If / cut in line / in front of me, / .

   If someone cut in line in front of me, I'd be angry.

2 in the library, / ask them to be quiet / people / were talking too loudly / If / I'd / .

   _____

3 If / I kept / "I'm sorry." / someone waiting / say, / I'd

   _____

4 I'd / if / be happy / gave me / a compliment, / someone / .

   _____

5 were dropping litter / What / if / would you do / your friend / out of your car / ?

   _____

6 you say / your parents / gave you / If / what / a lot of money, / would / ?

   _____

5 Circle the correct words to complete each question.

How polite are you?

1 What (would you do) / did you do if your friend **would talk / were talking** loudly at a movie?

2 If you **would see / saw** someone drop litter on the ground, what **would you say / did you say**?

3 If you **would like / liked** a stranger's jacket, **would you give / you gave** him or her a compliment?

4 What **would you do / did you do** if an elderly person **would need / needed** a seat on a train?

5 What **would you do / did you do** if your friend **asked / would ask** you for a lot of money?

6 If you **make / made** a mistake, **did you admit / would you admit** it?

7 If you **are / were** impatient to get your concert ticket, **would you cut / did you cut** in line?

8 What **would you do / did you do** if someone **would want / wanted** directions to a place in your town?

6 Answer the questions from Exercise 5 with your own information.

Example: I'd feel embarrassed, but I wouldn't say anything.

1 _____

2 _____

3 _____

4 _____

5 _____

6 _____

7 _____

8 _____

B I didn't realize that.

1 Complete the sentences with the correct words.

1 It's the custom_____ to leave a tip.

2 Oh, I d_____ k_____ that.

3 Oh, r_____? I wasn't a_____ of that.

4 You're s_____ to pay the waiter.

5 Really? I didn't r_____ that.

6 You're e_____ to leave 15 to 20 percent of the amount on the check.

2 Complete the conversation with the sentences from Exercise 1.
Sometimes more than one answer is possible.

Tracey   This food was great.

Yae Wan   I agree, and it wasn't very expensive.

It's $32, so that's $16 for me, and $16 for you.

Tracey   We need to give more than $32.

It's the custom to leave a tip_____ .

You know, some money for the waiter.

Yae Wan   _____ . We only do
                                    2

that in fancy restaurants in South Korea. Should we leave $34?

Tracey   No. That's not enough.

_____ .
                        3

Yae Wan   _____ . Let's leave
                                    4

20 percent. The waiter was great.

Tracey   OK. How much is that?

Yae Wan   Let's see . . . 20 percent of $32 is $6.40, so it's $38.40 total. Let's just

give $40. Do we pay at the front of the restaurant?

Tracey   No. _____ .
                            5

Yae Wan   _____ . OK, here
                                    6

he comes.

Tracey   Excuse me . . . We're ready to pay.

C Doing things differently

1 Cross out the word that doesn't belong in each list

1 **make**	a request	an excuse	~~a favor~~
2 **offer**	an apology	a request	an explanation
3 **ask for**	an explanation	a favor	a compromise
4 **accept**	an opinion	an apology	a compliment
5 **turn down**	a request	an invitation	an excuse

2 Circle the correct word(s) to complete each conversation.

1 **A** Jack told me he liked my new haircut.

   B Really? He doesn't **accept** /(**give**)

   compliments often.

2 **A** I think there's too much pollution in this city.

   B Really? **I disagree with / agree with** your

   opinion. It's much cleaner than a lot of cities

   that I've visited.

3 **A** Thanks for helping me with my homework.

   B No problem. I'm happy to **return / ask for** the favor. Remember that you

   helped me last week!

4 **A** I don't know if we'll ever agree. You want a lot of things I don't want.

   B Well, let's try to **suggest / reach** a compromise.

5 **A** Did you **accept / turn down** Mark's invitation to dinner?

   B Yes, I did. I have to stay home with the kids that night.

6 **A** Jenny kept me waiting for an hour yesterday.

   B Did you **ask her for / offer her** an explanation?

   A Yes, I did. She said she had to stay late at work to finish a report.

7 **A** I'd like to **turn down / make** a request for a window seat.

   B No problem, sir. You can sit in seat 14F. That's a window seat. Enjoy your flight.

3 Look at the pictures. Check (✓) TWO possible sentences for each picture.

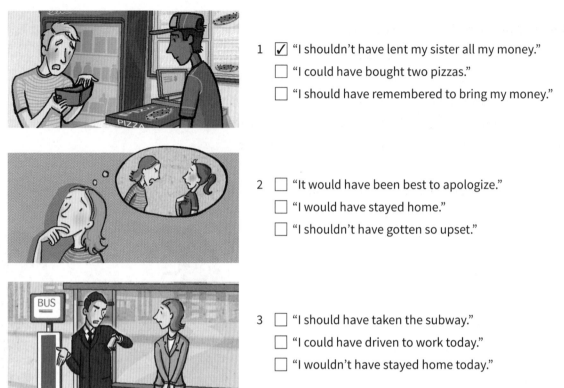

1 ☑ "I shouldn't have lent my sister all my money."
   ☐ "I could have bought two pizzas."
   ☐ "I should have remembered to bring my money."

2 ☐ "It would have been best to apologize."
   ☐ "I would have stayed home."
   ☐ "I shouldn't have gotten so upset."

3 ☐ "I should have taken the subway."
   ☐ "I could have driven to work today."
   ☐ "I wouldn't have stayed home today."

4 Write sentences with the words in parentheses and past modals.

1 (I / shouldn't / borrow / Julie's car)
   _I shouldn't have borrowed Julie's car_____ .

2 (What / could / I / do / differently)
   _____ ?

3 (I / could / take / the bus)
   _____ .

4 (I / should / drive / more slowly)
   _____ .

5 (Julie / wouldn't / drive / so fast)
   _____ .

6 (She / would / see / the stop sign)
   _____ .

7 (Should / I / offer to pay Julie / to fix the car)
   _____ ?

8 (What / would / you / do)
   _____ ?

5 Complete the letters with the correct form of the word pairs in the box.

could / give	could / microwave	✓ should / do	shouldn't / say

Dear Henry Helper,

My wife was really upset last night. She made a nice dinner, and I said that it was cold. I don't understand why she got so angry. It <u>was</u> cold! What <u>should</u>
                                                                    1
I <u>have done</u> ? –*Confused in Chicago*
      1

Dear Confused in Chicago,

Your wife made you a nice dinner. You _____ her
                                                    2
a compliment. You _____ the dinner was cold.
                              3
You _____ it to make it hot enough! –*Henry Helper*
           4

could / do	should / talk	would / reach	wouldn't / get

Dear Henry Helper,

My roommate and I often disagree. Last week, we argued about keeping the kitchen clean. We're not talking to each other now. What _____ we
                                                                    5
_____ differently? –*Angry Anita*
            5

Dear Angry Anita,

I _____ so upset. You and your roommate
              6
_____ about the problem quietly. It's important
              7
for roommates to work together, so I _____ a
                                                          8
compromise. Try to stay relaxed the next time you don't agree. A dirty kitchen isn't a good reason to lose a friend! –*Henry Helper*

6 Look at the letters in Exercise 5. Write responses with your own ideas. Use past modals.

Example: <u>I wouldn't have said anything.</u> *or* <u>You could have said thank you.</u>

1 Dear Confused in Chicago,

_____

2 Dear Angry Anita,

_____

D Acts of kindness

1 Read the article. In what places does the Random Acts of Kindness Foundation try to inspire kindness?

Something to
THINK ABOUT

The Random Acts of Kindness Foundation is an organization that inspires people to be kind. It started in 1995, and its goal is to spread kindness. The people of the Foundation want us to be kind to others. And if someone is kind to you, they want you to "pay it forward" by doing something nice for someone else. Their website gives people ideas on how to be kind in schools and at work.

People post ideas on the Foundation website about ways to be kind. Several people have posted ways they are kind at work. A manager at a company in Texas brings cake to work for each employee's birthday. A manager at a company in California had a "Not-Going-Away" pizza party. She said that they used to celebrate only when people left the company. She decided to have a "Not-Going-Away" party for the employees who worked there and didn't leave. It was fun, and the employees felt appreciated. Another manager in Illinois bought a vacation apartment for her employees. They get points for good things

they do at work, and each weekend one of her 45 employees uses the apartment. They take family or friends for a weekend vacation.

Some companies inspire employees to do kind things for each other. One company has "Secret Pals." Each employee fills out information about his or her interests and hobbies, and the information is given to another employee who is their "Secret Pal." The Secret Pal does kind things for the other person, like giving them gifts or kind notes. The employees know the person they are doing kind things for, but they don't know who is doing kind things for them. Another company in Iowa sold bags of candy and flowers to their employees. The employees bought the candy and flowers and gave them to each other. It was a way for employees to give each other small gifts to say thank you. The company made over $700. They could have kept the money, but they "paid it forward," and gave the money to a charity.

2 Read the text again. Then check (✓) the items that are random acts of kindness mentioned in the reading.
1 ☐ posting ideas on a website
2 ☑ bringing cake for people's birthdays
3 ☐ having a Not-Going-Away party for employees
4 ☐ going on vacation
5 ☐ giving a small gift to someone at work
6 ☐ giving money to charity

Travel and tourism

A Cities

1 Complete Wendy's notes about her vacation. Use the correct words from the box.

culturally diverse	highly educated	slow-paced
densely populated	high-tech	well-planned
fun-loving	open-minded	✓ world-famous

October 7: I'm traveling in South America!
Right now I'm in Quito, Ecuador. It's a
beautiful and mountainous city. Yesterday, I
went to the ___world-famous___ place
1

called Mitad del Mundo. I met people from
all over — France, Canada, Brazil, and
more! Mitad del Mundo means the middle of
the world. I had one foot in the northern half
of the world and one in the southern half!
Last week, I was in Guayaquil. It's a
_____ city. People like to
2

dance, and there are parties in the streets
after soccer games!

October 10: Colombia is amazing!
Yesterday, I flew to Bogotá. Bogotá is a
very _____ city.
3

There are so many people here!

Tomorrow, I'm going to the rain forest.
It will be _____
4

compared to Bogotá. I'm going to relax
there, but I'll also learn a lot about the
environment from the people who live in
the rain forest.

October 15: I'm in Brazil now. Portuguese,
not Spanish, is spoken here. Right now I'm
in Curtiba. It's a _____
5

city. There is a great bus system, and there
are bus stops next to most of the important
buildings. There are also many parks here.
It's a _____ city, and
6

many of the parks have items from different
cultures in them. The people here are
_____ . There are many
7

universities in the city.

October 28: Now I'm in Santiago, Chile.
It's the most _____ city
8

I've visited. It seems like there are startup
technology companies everywhere. The
people are _____ .
9

They like to talk about different ideas,
opinions, and experiences. People speak
Spanish, English, and German here.

2 Write sentences with the words in parentheses and the comparative form of the adjectives (+ *more*, – *less*, = *as . . . as*, ≠ *not as . . . as*).

1 (Seattle / wet + / Las Vegas)
   Seattle is wetter than Las Vegas.

2 (New Orleans / slow-paced + / New York)

3 (Kyoto / expensive – / Tokyo)

4 (Small cities / usually / dangerous ≠ / big cities)

5 (The subway system / good + / the buses / in this city)

6 (The international restaurants / bad + / the traditional restaurants / in this town)

7 (Paris / famous = / New York City / for its great museums)

3 Complete the text with the superlative form of the words in parentheses.

Homer, Alaska, is one of my favorite cities. It's a slow-paced city, and it's

___*the most relaxing*___ (relaxing) city I've ever visited.
₁

It was _____ (stressful) vacation I've
₂

ever had. I had a lot of time to myself, and I felt very calm. Homer isn't very

densely populated. There are only about 145 people per square kilometer. The

mornings are _____ (busy) time of
₃

the day because many people fish in the mornings. The restaurants in Homer

have some of _____ (delicious) seafood in the
₄

world. There was only one thing I didn't like. I had problems

getting to Homer. In fact, it was _____ (bad)
₅

travel experience I've ever had! But I still think Homer is

_____ (good) city in Alaska.
₆

4 Circle the correct word(s) to complete each conversation.

1 **A** What's _____ city in the world?

  B I don't know, but I think it might be Bangkok. When I was there, it was very hot.

    a hottest   b hotter than   (c) the hottest

2 **A** What's the biggest city in the world? Is it New York City?

  B No, many cities are _____ New York, like Tokyo or Mexico City.

    a bigger than   b the biggest   c big

3 **A** Did you know that Mumbai is _____ Tokyo?

  B No. That's really interesting. It must have a very large population.

    a the most densely populated   b more densely populated than   c the least densely populated

4 **A** Hesperia is one of _____ cities in California.

  B Really? Maybe I'll move there. Los Angeles is so expensive!

    a less expensive than   b the least expensive   c cheaper than

5 **A** New York is the best city in the United States!

  B I disagree. I think Chicago is _____ New York.

    a better than   b the best   c better

6 **A** What's _____ city in the world?

  B I think it's Seoul. I read that somewhere before.

    a less high-tech than   b more high-tech than   c the most high-tech

5 Look at the chart. Then answer the questions. Use complete sentences.

	Quito	Sapporo	Seoul
Size	372 square km	1,700 square km	605 square km
Population density	7,200 per square km	1,121 per square km	17,000 per square km
January average temperature	13°C	−4°C	0°C
August average temperature	14°C	22°C	29°C

1 Which city is bigger – Sapporo or Seoul? _Sapporo is bigger than Seoul._

2 Which city is the smallest? _____

3 Which city is the most densely populated? _____

4 Which city is warmer in January – Sapporo or Seoul? _____

5 Which city is the coolest in August? _____

B I'll let someone know.

1 Read the sentences and check (✓) the correct column.

		Reporting a problem	Responding to a problem
1	There's a problem with this pasta.	✓	☐
2	I'll let someone know right away.	☐	☐
3	I'm having a problem with my menu.	☐	☐
4	There seems to be a problem with our food.	☐	☐
5	I'll get someone to take care of it.	☐	☐
6	I'll have someone get on it right away.	☐	☐

2 Complete the conversations with the sentences from Exercise 1. Sometimes more than one answer is possible.

A. **Carl**   Excuse me . . .

    <u>There's a problem with this pasta.</u>
                  1

   Waiter What's wrong with it?

   Carl   It's cold!

   Waiter I'm sorry. _____
                      2

              _____
                      3

   Carl   Thank you.

B. **Isabella** Uh, hello . . . Can you help me?

   Waiter   Of course. What's the problem?

   Isabella _____
                    1
             Look! It's in French. I can't read it.

   Waiter   _____
                    2

C. **Truong** Excuse me . . . _____
                         1

   Waiter What is it?

   Truong Well, I asked for it an hour ago, and it's not here!

   Waiter I'm sorry. _____
                      2

C Travel experiences

1 Complete the puzzle with the correct words that complete the sentences.

Across

3 This restaurant is _____ . I can't believe it got five stars. I'd give it two!

5 When I went to Seoul, I was _____ to first class!

7 Our hotel was _____ , but the manager found us a room in another hotel.

8 The museums in Spain are usually _____ on the weekends. They're less crowded during the week.

9 Paul's flight to Vancouver was _____ for two hours. He worked on his laptop while he waited.

Down

1 My ticket to Australia was $3,120! I know it's expensive to fly there, but I think my ticket was _____ .

2 I was _____ a seat on the train, but when I got there, my seat was taken.

4 We got a _____ price on our airline tickets, but the hotels were expensive.

6 My visa _____ last year, and I haven't gotten a new one yet.

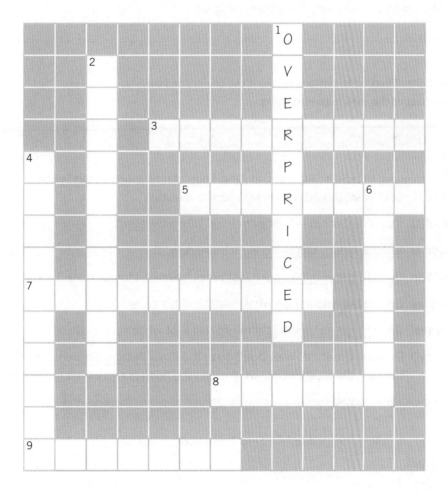

2 Jill is planning her trip. Put her words in the correct order to make sentences.

1 Thomas / to / me / that was priced right / told / find a ticket / .
   Thomas told me to find a ticket that was priced right.

2 advised / upgrade / at the airport / Pam / me / to / my ticket / .
   _____

3 a discounted ticket / Seth / reminded / to buy / me / .
   _____

4 let my visa / expire / not / me / to / reminded / Isabel / .
   _____

5 travel alone / not / advised / My grandmother / me / to / .
   _____

6 at night / She / to / me / take / not / the subway / warned / .
   _____

3 Look at the website. Then write sentences about the underlined advice.
Use the simple past of the verb in parentheses.

Hi friends! I'm going to Sydney, Australia, in June. I don't know much about Sydney.
What should I pack? What should I do there? Thanks! –Heather

JaneB92 It isn't very warm in Sydney in June. Take a sweater!

MelvinJones See the Sydney Opera House! It's amazing.

Ahmet1986 Don't forget your passport! Last time I traveled, I forgot mine. I missed my flight!

LingLee Do you like wildlife? Go whale watching. It's incredible!

LoriTravel Don't forget an umbrella. It might rain a lot while you are there.

FreddyD Do you like nature? Well, don't go to the Royal Botanic Gardens. I think you should go hiking in the Blue Mountains. You can see flowers and plants in the mountains.

1 (Jane / advise)   Jane advised her to take a sweater.
2 (Melvin / advise)   _____
3 (Ahmet / warn)   _____
4 (Ling / tell)   _____
5 (Lori / remind)   _____
6 (Freddy / tell)   _____

4 Mateo and Pilar are talking on the phone and will meet at the airport. Write what they said. Use reporting verbs.

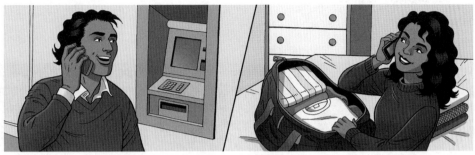

1 **Mateo**   "Pilar, use the big bags for the clothes."

   (advise)   Mateo advised Pilar to use the big bags for the clothes.

2 **Pilar**   "Mateo, bring enough cash."

   (remind) _____

3 **Mateo**   "Pilar, remember the passports."

   (tell) _____

4 **Pilar**   "Mateo, don't forget to pick up our tickets."

   (remind) _____

5 **Mateo**   "Pilar, don't forget to lock the doors!"

   (tell) _____

6 **Pilar**   "Mateo, don't be late to the airport!"

   (warn) _____

5 What commands or advice have people given you in the past? Use reporting verbs with your own ideas or some of the expressions from the box.

Example: ___My friend reminded me to take an umbrella on my trip to Seattle.___ *or*
            ___My mother warned me not to stay out late.___

be careful driving	get a visa	not stay out late
call someone	not forget something	remember a key to something
do your homework	not go out alone	take something on vacation

1 _____

2 _____

3 _____

4 _____

5 _____

6 _____

D My town, the best town

1 **Read the travel information. Then answer the questions.**

1 Which city is colder in the winter? _____.

2 Which city is warmer in the summer? _____.

Moscow, Russia
Moscow is a world-famous city with many sights to see. You'll want to spend at least a week here.

Geography and Population: Moscow is 130 meters above sea level. The population is 10.5 million with about 9,800 people per square kilometer.

Climate: The average temperature is –5°C in the winter and 16°C in the summer.

Getting around: The worst way to get around Moscow is by car. Take the subway (called the Metro) or a bus or tram instead. The Metro is usually faster.

Things to see and do: Moscow has many museums, and you can visit historic sites like the Bolshoi Theater, the most famous theater in Russia. There are also many parks. Don't forget to take a boat trip on the Moscow River!

For more information, call 1-800-555-4310 or visit www.visitmoscow/cup.com.

Moscow, Idaho, the United States
Moscow is a safe and friendly town in Idaho. All seasons are beautiful, and it's an easy getaway for a weekend trip.

Geography and Population: Moscow is 786 meters above sea level in a mountainous area. It is a small town with a population of about 23,000 and about 1,440 people per square kilometer.

Climate: The average temperature in the winter is 2°C, and in summer it is 18°C.

Getting around: The best way to get around in Moscow is to drive. You can also call the Dial-A-Ride bus company to pick you up and take you where you want to go.

Things to see and do: In the summer, Moscow is a great place to hike and ride bikes. In the winter, you can ski or ride snowmobiles. Every February, Moscow hosts a jazz festival.

For more information, call 1-866-555-6000 or visit www.travelmoscowus/cup.com.

2 **Read the travel information again. Then read the sentences and write where each person went. Write *Russia* or *the United States*.**

1 Susan went to the city that is higher above sea level.   the United States

2 Carlos went to the city that has fewer people. _____

3 Ji Sung and Lilly took the subway around the city. _____

4 Bianca went to a concert in a famous theater. _____

4 Dan and Ken went to a music festival in February. _____

5 Marcia and Mel took a boat trip on a river. _____

The way we are

A Who I am

1 Put the letters in the correct order to make words for character traits.

1 y o l a l   _loyal_

2 c e g r e e n t i _____

3 a i l d t e i i s c _____

4 a l l g i o c   _____

5 d u u s o i s t   _____

6 v c i e p t m i o t e   _____

7 e a t m i a i i g n v   _____

8 n n d d e e i p n e t   _____

9 r s u e b l l e i o   _____

2 Daisuke is going to meet Yumiko's family. Complete the conversation with words for character traits.

Daisuke So, Yumiko, what is your family like?

Yumiko Well, my parents are great. They're very

_____ _loyal_ _____ . They always

_____ 1

support me! My older sister is an artist.

She's very _____ and
_____ 2

has a lot of interesting ideas. She can also

be very _____ .
_____ 3

She thinks her art is going to save the world!

Daisuke That's funny! What's your younger sister like?

Yumiko She's great, too, but we're very _____ . I'm only a year
_____ 4

older than she is. We both want to be the best player on our soccer team.

Daisuke My brother and I are like that, too, especially with math. We're both _____
_____ 5

when we make decisions, too. But he's more _____ than I am. I don't spend
_____ 6

very much time studying.

Yumiko I know! Maybe that's why you're always so _____ !
_____ 7

I never have energy at school because I stay up so late studying.

Daisuke Anyway, tell me about your brother. What's he like?

Yumiko He's nice, but he's very _____ . He's 21, and he doesn't
_____ 8

do a lot with the family now. When he was younger, he was pretty _____
_____ 9

and didn't want to follow the rules.

3 Complete the sentences with *who* or *which*.

1 Danielle is the kind of person _____who_____ likes to be with her family.

2 Her parents are people _____ are very energetic.

3 They took a vacation _____ was very adventurous.

4 Danielle has a brother _____ is pretty rebellious.

5 She has a sister _____ is sensitive and quiet.

6 Her sister has a job _____ is difficult.

7 She works in an office _____ is often busy.

8 Danielle has a lot of friends _____ enjoy coming to her house.

4 Rewrite the sentences about Lea and Omar. Change *that* to *who* or *which*.

1 Lea and Omar have a house that is near the ocean.

   Lea and Omar have a house which is near the ocean.

2 Lea is someone that loves the ocean.

   _____

3 But Omar is the kind of person that doesn't like the water.

   _____

4 They have a boat that he never uses.

   _____

5 Omar is a person that likes to play golf.

   _____

6 Lea and Omar are people that don't always do things together.

   _____

5 Read the text and look at the underlined pronouns. Cross out the pronouns that are optional.

My friend Paul is a person ~~who~~ other students want to work with. He has personality traits <u>that</u> people like. For example, he's the kind of student <u>that</u> usually knows the answers to the teacher's questions, and he's someone <u>who</u> always finishes his work. He's also a person <u>who</u> doesn't mind helping his classmates with their work.

Outside of class, Paul is a person <u>who</u> is a good friend. People say he's a friend <u>that</u> they can talk to. Paul is also the kind of person <u>who</u> is interested in a lot of things. He's a great musician. The instrument <u>that</u> he plays best is the guitar, but he plays the piano, too. He's the kind of musician <u>that</u> I want to be!

6 Check (✓) TWO phrases that can complete each sentence.

1 Burak has imaginative ideas . . .
- ✓ that are hard to understand.
- ✓ which are useful for his job.
- ☐ who is also logical.

2 My parents are energetic people . . .
- ☐ that like adventure.
- ☐ are idealistic.
- ☐ who do many interesting things.

3 Penelope is a person . . .
- ☐ teachers like.
- ☐ is my best friend.
- ☐ who sings really well.

4 TSmart is a new smartphone . . .
- ☐ that I have to have.
- ☐ has a 3D screen.
- ☐ people are buying.

5 Chicago is a city . . .
- ☐ people travel to for fun.
- ☐ that gets a lot of snow.
- ☐ who is very windy.

6 I have a lot of friends . . .
- ☐ who are loyal.
- ☐ want to be musicians.
- ☐ that like to be independent.

7 Complete the sentences with your own ideas. Use *who, which,* or *that*.

Example: I like cities __that are exciting__ . *or* I like cities __which are small and quiet__ .

1 I like cities _____ .

2 I dislike people _____ .

3 I want a job _____ .

4 A loyal person is someone _____ .

B Sorry, but can I ask something?

Complete the conversation with the correct words.

Paulo   Listen to this. This article says your favorite color says a lot about your personality.

Amelia   Really? What does it say?

Paulo   Well, first tell me your favorite color.

Amelia   It's yellow.

Paulo   OK, it says you are idealistic. It also says . . .

Amelia   Sorry _____ , but c_____ I ask s_____ ?
                         1   1   1

Paulo   Y_____ , of c_____ .
                         2   2

Amelia   What does it mean by idealistic?

Paulo   You know, you're determined to make good things happen.

Amelia   Oh, OK. What else does it say?

Paulo   It says you are good at making plans, but you're often not energetic enough to do them. And it says . . .

Amelia   B_____ you g_____ on, could I a_____ something?
                         3   3   3

Paulo   OK. S_____ .
                         4

Amelia   What magazine is this from? It sounds kind of crazy.

Paulo   It's a psychology magazine. Let me tell you more. It says . . .

Amelia   I'm sorry, b_____ could I ask o_____ t_____ ?
                         5   5   5

Paulo   You mean, one more thing? Sure. G_____ a_____ .
                                                        6   6

Amelia   What's the name of the magazine?

Paulo   *Modern Psychology.* OK, now let me finish. It says you are logical and you like to know the facts. Now, doesn't that sound like you?

Amelia   Well, yes, but . . .

C Wishing for change

1 Label each picture with a sentence made from the correct phrase from the box.

balance work and play	find time to relax	live within a budget
be more organized	lead a healthier lifestyle	✓ manage time better

1 He needs to manage time better.

2 _____

3 _____

4 _____

5 _____

6 _____

2 Answer the questions with your own information.

Example: *I try to do something fun for an hour every day after work.*

1 How do you balance work and play?

_____

2 Do you manage your time well? How could you manage your time better?

_____

3 Do you usually live within your budget? How could you save more money?

_____

4 Do you find time to relax during the week? What's your favorite way to relax?

_____

5 Are you more organized at work or at home? What could you do to be more organized?

_____

6 Do you lead a healthy lifestyle? What could you do to be healthier?

_____

3 Match each situation with the correct wish.

1 I can't find anything in my office! ___f___
2 I can't go to the concert with you. _____
3 I'm really thirsty. _____
4 I never feel like exercising. _____
5 I don't understand how this puzzle works. _____
6 I really like music. _____
7 I only got 34% on my history test. _____
8 I got so angry when we lost the soccer game. _____

a I wish I didn't have plans on Friday.
b I wish I were more energetic.
c I wish I weren't so competitive.
d I wish I had a glass of water.
e I wish I could take it again.
f I wish I could be more organized.
g I wish I could play an instrument.
h I wish I were more logical.

4 Circle the correct word to complete each wish.

Top Ten Wishes

What do you wish for? We took a survey and here are the top results. Have you ever said any of these things?

1 "I wish I **travel** / (**could travel**) around the world."

2 "I wish I **had** / **have** a new car."

3 "I wish I **were** / **am** rich."

4 "I wish I **not have** / **didn't have** to work."

5 "I wish I **weren't** / **were** so stressed."

6 "I wish I **can see** / **could see** my future."

7 "I wish I **live** / **lived** within a budget."

8 "I wish I **could lost** / **could lose** weight."

9 "I wish I **were** / **are** healthier."

10 "I wish I **didn't spend** / **don't spend** so much money."

5 Read the sentences. Write wishes with the opposite information.

1 I'm not imaginative. _I wish I were imaginative._

2 My sister is extremely talkative. _I wish my sister weren't._

3 My travel budget is small. _____

4 I'm not studious. _____

5 My soccer team isn't competitive. _____

6 I'm always busy on weekends. _____

6 Read the sentences. Write complete sentences with your own information.

Example: _I wish I could read fast._

1 Write two things you wish you could do.

_____

_____

2 Write two things you wish you had.

_____

_____

3 Write two personality traits you wish you had or didn't have.

_____

_____

D Alternative therapies

1 Read the text. What is the name of the job for a person who uses music to help people?

_____

Music Heals

Music therapy is using music to help people with a variety of problems. For example, it can help people with communication and speech problems speak better. It can help people with memory problems remember things from their past. Music therapy can also help people manage stress and be more relaxed. It can even make people with bad pain feel better.

In music therapy, a music therapist works with one person alone or with small groups. The therapist meets with the person and does tests to find out what the problem is and what the person can do with music. Then the therapist decides what kind of music therapy to use. Some people sing, and others might compose music, but a person doesn't need to know about music to be helped by music therapy. There are options such as listening to music and dancing to music. Research shows that these activities are good for the body and for the mind.

Homes that take care of elderly people often have music therapy programs. The programs help the elderly be more energetic and also help with memory problems. Some hospitals have music therapy for patients who are in a lot of pain. Music can affect a part of the brain that reduces pain.

Trevor Gibbons is one example of a person who was helped by music therapy. In 2000, he was putting in windows on the fourth floor of a building when he fell. He was in the hospital for over a year. He was in a lot of pain, and he couldn't talk. He went from the hospital to a rehabilitation center that has a music therapy program, and a music therapist worked with him for several years. He could sing more easily than he could talk. Trevor says that music also helped him manage loneliness, sadness, and pain after he was hurt. Music and the music therapist inspired him, and he has written and sung many songs. He has even recorded CDs and performed at Lincoln Center in New York.

2 Read the text again. Then write T (true), F (false), or NI (no information).

1 Music therapy can help people with many different problems. ____T____

2 You do not have to be good at music to benefit from music therapy. _____

3 Music therapy is only for very old people. _____

4 Music therapy didn't help Trevor with his pain. _____

5 It took Trevor five years to get better. _____